Corinna LAUGHLIN

The Martyrs of La Florida

A HEROIC STORY OF CATHOLIC FAITH

Éditions du Signe

Publisher :

Éditions du Signe
1, rue Alfred Kastler
BP 98094 Eckbolsheim
67038 Strasbourg Cedex - FRANCE
Tel.: (011 +33) 3 88 78 91 91 - Fax: (011 +33) 3 88 78 91 99
www.editionsdusigne.fr
e-mail: info@editionsdusigne.fr

President and Publishing Director: **Christian RIEHL**
Director of Publications: **Dr. Claude-Bernard COSTECALDE**

Production Manager: **Marc de JONG**

Text: **Corinna LAUGHLIN**
Illustrator: **André LE BRAS**
Coloring: **Christophe GIBELIN, Paolo FRANCESCUTTO**

ISBN: 978-2-7468-3616-7 (111231) - softcover
978-2-7468-3867-3 (111671) - hardcover

Printed in Serbia

October 4, 2019

Dear Reader,

On January 26, 1704, a Native American man named Antonio was tied to a large cross at the mission of La Concepción de Ayubale, near modern-day Tallahassee, and burned to death. This beloved and capable leader of the Apalachee people was burned alive from sunrise to sunset on that winter day. All the while he suffered, he spoke in native tongues with boldness from his cross. Rather than the customary words vowing vengeance on his captors, Antonio preached his faith in God and warned his tormentors about their sin. Antonio longed to be with God in heaven. An apparition of the Blessed Virgin Mary sustained him in his final moments. It was her eyes, he said, which gave him strength.

The story of the martyrs of *La Florida* is a tale that, in its own time, resounded through the Church. Word spread of Fr. Luis Cáncer walking unarmed and with perfect knowledge toward his death; of Antonia, the teenaged daughter of the Spanish governor, tied to a bell tower and proclaiming her faith so fearlessly that her angered captors removed her tongue; of the young Native American altar server and chief, who preferred to die rather than renounce his faith. Such a story could not be contained. Faithful priests and Christian natives perished in the distant woods of *La Florida*, yet their stories reached the desks of bishops, kings, and popes, from Cuba, to Mexico, to Spain, and to Rome. Some stories were reverently retold by religious orders committed to preserving their brothers' memories, while other stories fell prey to the obscurity of years and were nearly forgotten.

Some of the stories presented here reflect the careful research of scholars working over the course of many decades in archives throughout Europe and the Americas. When possible, the scholars working on this canonization effort have handled and studied these archival sources at length. Other stories presented here are substantiated by documents of which at the moment only transcriptions exist. The research for this cause continues! I encourage you to marvel at the faith of those whose stories have already been confirmed beyond the slightest doubt and to appreciate the holy courage of the hundreds of Native Americans about whom we pray time will permit us to speak with greater assurance.

Even as we introduce you to the well-attested tale of *La Florida*, we invite you to join us with your prayers on this journey of patient research and historical recovery which began hundreds of years ago and has not yet reached its end.

Sincerely,

+William A. Wack

Bishop William A. Wack, CSC
Pensacola-Tallahassee

PRAYER FOR THE BEATIFICATION OF SERVANTS OF GOD ANTONIO CUIPA AND COMPANIONS

O GOD, FATHER OF ALL NATIONS,
YOU HAVE SUMMONED US TO ANNOUNCE THE FREEDOM OF YOUR CHILDREN.
WE THANK YOU FOR CALLING YOUR SERVANTS, ANTONIO CUIPA AND HIS COMPANIONS,
TO PROCLAIM THE CATHOLIC FAITH DURING THE BIRTH OF A NEW NATION.
MAY THEIR EXAMPLE OF SUFFERING AND FORGIVENESS GIVE US THE COURAGE
TO BEAR WITNESS TO CHRIST IN OUR OWN TIME.
WE ALSO PRAY THAT THEY BE COUNTED ONE DAY AMONG YOUR SAINTS.
THROUGH THE INTERCESSION OF YOUR SERVANTS, GRANT US THE FOLLOWING GRACE
WHICH WE ASK FROM YOUR LOVING KINDNESS

{HERE MAKE YOUR REQUEST}

WE ASK THIS THROUGH CHRIST, OUR LORD. AMEN

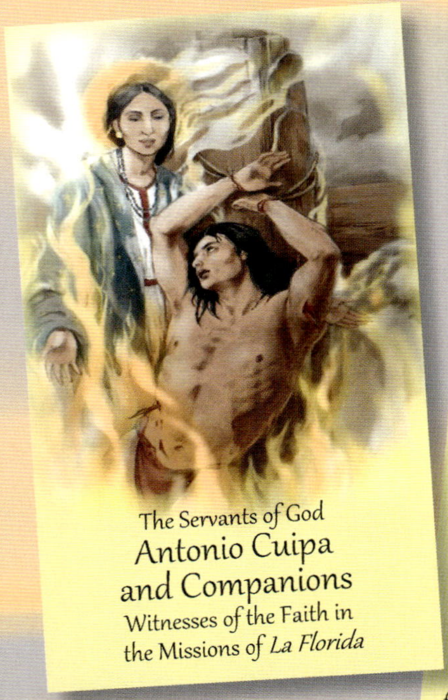

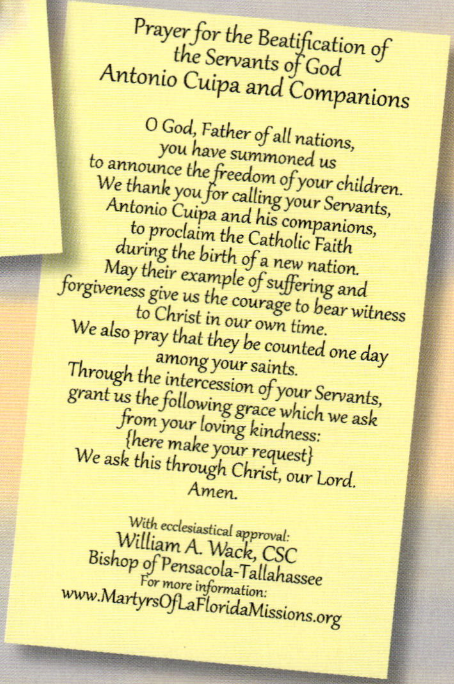
Prayer for the Beatification of
the Servants of God
Antonio Cuipa and Companions

O God, Father of all nations,
you have summoned us
to announce the freedom of your children.
We thank you for calling your Servants,
Antonio Cuipa and his companions,
to proclaim the Catholic Faith
during the birth of a new nation.
May their example of suffering and
forgiveness give us the courage to bear witness
to Christ in our own time.
We also pray that they be counted one day
among your saints.
Through the intercession of your Servants,
grant us the following grace which we ask
from your loving kindness:
{here make your request}
We ask this through Christ, our Lord.
Amen.

With ecclesiastical approval:
William A. Wack, CSC
Bishop of Pensacola-Tallahassee
For more information:
www.MartyrsOfLaFloridaMissions.org

To report prayers answered or favors granted through the intercession of Antonio & the Martyrs of *La Florida*, please contact secretary@martyrsoflafloridamissions.org

LONG BEFORE ENGLISH COLONISTS CAME ASHORE AT JAMESTOWN ISLAND...
BEFORE THE PILGRIMS ARRIVED AT PLYMOUTH ROCK...
BEFORE A WAR WAS FOUGHT FOR INDEPENDENCE...
BEFORE A NATION STRETCHED FROM "SEA TO SHINING SEA"...
PEOPLE LIVED AND DIED FOR THE CATHOLIC FAITH IN WHAT IS NOW THE SOUTHEASTERN UNITED STATES: FLORIDA, GEORGIA, ALABAMA, SOUTH CAROLINA, AND AS FAR NORTH AS VIRGINIA. OVER MORE THAN TWO CENTURIES, FROM 1549 UNTIL 1761, HUNDREDS WERE MARTYRED FOR THEIR FAITH IN CHRIST. THEY WERE NATIVE AMERICANS AND EUROPEANS, RELIGIOUS AND LAYPERSONS, CHIEFS AND COMMONERS, SOLDIERS AND CIVILIANS, MEN AND WOMEN, YOUNG AND OLD. THIS IS THEIR STORY.
MAP
OF FLORIDA

BEFORE THE COMING OF EUROPEANS, THERE WERE MANY LANGUAGES AND MANY CULTURES IN THIS LAND... TIMUCUA.... MUSCOGEE... YAMASEE... APALACHEE... AND MANY MORE.
NATIVE AMERICANS WERE RESOURCEFUL HUNTERS, FISHERS, AND GATHERERS...
THEY WERE FIERCE WARRIORS.
THEY LIVED IN HARMONY WITH THE CYCLES OF THE WORLD.
SOME TRIBES MIGRATED SEASONALLY, FOLLOWING THE ABUNDANCE OF PLANTS, FISH, AND ANIMALS WITH THE CHANGING OF THE SEASONS.
OTHERS TILLED THE LAND, GROWING CORN, PUMPKINS, AND OTHER VEGETABLES. THEY DID NOT MOVE AROUND, BUT SETTLED IN LARGE AND THRIVING VILLAGES.
THE NATIVE PEOPLES HAD RICH CULTURES WITH ARTS AND CRAFTS, SPORTS, AND DIPLOMACY. THEY WERE WEAVERS, BUILDERS, AND HEALERS. THEY TRADED WITH OTHER TRIBES AS FAR AWAY AS THE GREAT LAKES. BUT EVERYTHING WAS ABOUT TO CHANGE.

1513. JUAN PONCE DE LEÓN BECAME THE FIRST EUROPEAN TO EXPLORE THIS REGION.
THIS IS EASTER WEEK... SO WE SHALL NAME THIS LAND PASCUA FLORIDA. THANKS BE TO GOD, WHO HAS PERMITTED ME TO SEE THIS BEAUTIFUL LAND FILLED WITH FLOWERS.

IN 1527, PÁNFILO DE NARVÁEZ SET FORTH FROM SPAIN WITH A FLEET OF SHIPS BOUND FOR LA FLORIDA.
WE HAVE OUR COMMISSION, MEN: TO CLAIM THIS NEW WORLD IN THE NAME OF KING CARLOS, AND TO ESTABLISH SETTLEMENTS. THERE ARE RICHES AND GOLD HERE, AND WE ARE GOING TO FIND THEM.
FRANCISCANS AND DIOCESAN PRIESTS ACCOMPANIED THE MISSION... THEIR DREAM WAS TO BRING THE GOSPEL TO THE NATIVE PEOPLES.
BUT THE EXPEDITION WAS ILL-FATED.
APRIL 12, 1528. (PRESENT-DAY TAMPA BAY)
LAND!
I HEREBY CLAIM THIS LAND FOR SPAIN, AND I BEG AND ANNOUNCE TO ALL INHABITANTS OF THIS LAND THAT THEY MUST ACKNOWLEDGE THE HOLY CATHOLIC CHURCH AND THE SUPREME PONTIFF AND LISTEN TO THE TEACHINGS OF THE FATHERS.

NARVÁEZ LED A DETACHMENT OF SOLDIERS TO EXPLORE THE LAND. THEY WERE SOON SEPARATED FROM THE FLEET-LOST, TIRED, AND HUNGRY.
WE MUST TAKE COVER!
STARVING AND WEARY, THE EXPEDITION FINALLY REACHED THE VILLAGES OF THE APALACHEE PEOPLE.
HAVE YOU FOUND ANY GOLD?
WE'VE FOUND SOMETHING BETTER-LOOK!
THE SURVIVORS BUILT SMALL BOATS AND DEPARTED.
BUT THEY WOULD SOON RETURN. IN 1539, HERNANDO DE SOTO LANDED AT WHAT IS NOW TAMPA BAY WITH NINE SHIPS AND OVER 600 MEN.
THEY SAY THESE TRIBES ARE UNCONQUERABLE. WE WILL SHOW THEM THE MIGHT OF SPAIN!

EARLY 1500S.... SPAIN.
HURRICANES, ROCKY SHOALS, DANGERS OF EVERY KIND...
I'VE HEARD THAT THE PEOPLE THERE ARE FIERCE BEYOND DESCRIPTION!
RICHES BEYOND OUR IMAGINATION, IF WE COULD JUST FIND THEM...
THE PEOPLE OF THE NEW WORLD NEED SOMEONE TO TEACH THEM ABOUT JESUS CHRIST!
FATHER LUIS CÁNCER, OP, A YOUNG DOMINICAN PRIEST, VOLUNTEERED TO GO TO THE NEW WORLD. HE WORKED ALONGSIDE BARTOLOMÉ DE LAS CASAS, WHO HAD BEEN GIVEN THE TITLE OF PROTECTOR OF THE INDIANS BY KING CARLOS OF SPAIN.
I AM EAGER TO BEGIN, TO TEACH THE PEOPLE THE WAYS OF JESUS.
FATHER CÁNCER, WE MUST LEARN AS WELL AS TEACH. I HAVE COME TO UNDERSTAND THAT THE GOSPEL MUST BE PREACHED TO THESE PEOPLE WITH LOVE AND GENTLENESS, NOT WITH MILITARY MIGHT.
WE MUST GO TO THEM WITHOUT WEAPONS, WITHOUT FEAR, BRINGING NOTHING BUT THE CROSS AND THE GOSPEL OF JESUS CHRIST.
WE MUST ENCOUNTER THEM WITH MEEKNESS, NOT WITH PRIDE.
AS LONG AS WE TRUST IN HUMAN STRENGTH, OUR EFFORTS WILL FAIL. BUT IF WE TRUST IN GOD...

* "THE LAND OF WAR," "THE LAND OF TRUE PEACE."

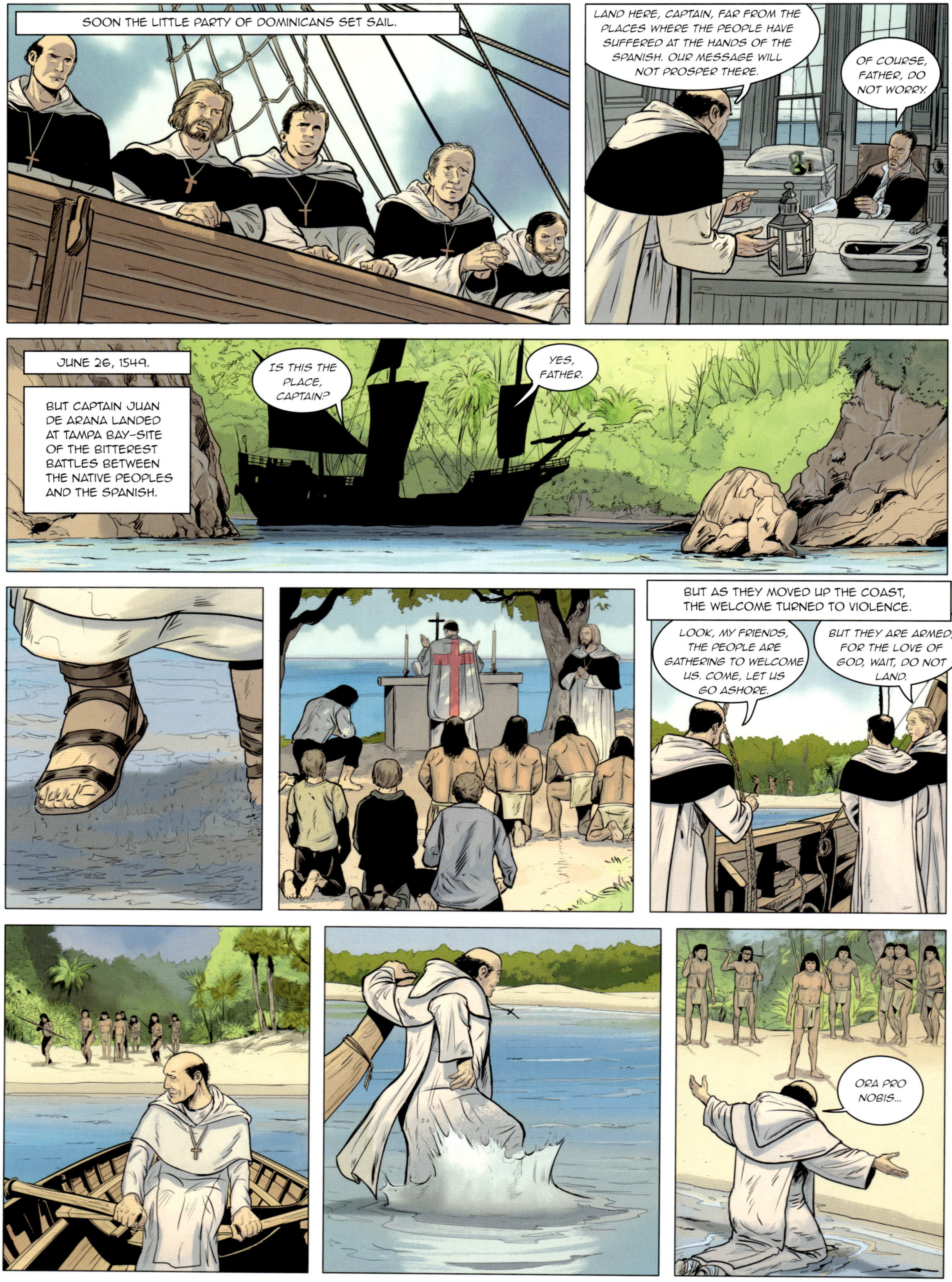
SOON THE LITTLE PARTY OF DOMINICANS SET SAIL.
LAND HERE, CAPTAIN, FAR FROM THE PLACES WHERE THE PEOPLE HAVE SUFFERED AT THE HANDS OF THE SPANISH. OUR MESSAGE WILL NOT PROSPER THERE.
OF COURSE, FATHER, DO NOT WORRY.
JUNE 26, 1549.
BUT CAPTAIN JUAN DE ARANA LANDED AT TAMPA BAY-SITE OF THE BITTEREST BATTLES BETWEEN THE NATIVE PEOPLES AND THE SPANISH.
IS THIS THE PLACE, CAPTAIN?
YES, FATHER.
BUT AS THEY MOVED UP THE COAST, THE WELCOME TURNED TO VIOLENCE.
LOOK, MY FRIENDS, THE PEOPLE ARE GATHERING TO WELCOME US. COME, LET US GO ASHORE.
BUT THEY ARE ARMED; FOR THE LOVE OF GOD, WAIT, DO NOT LAND.
ORA PRO NOBIS...

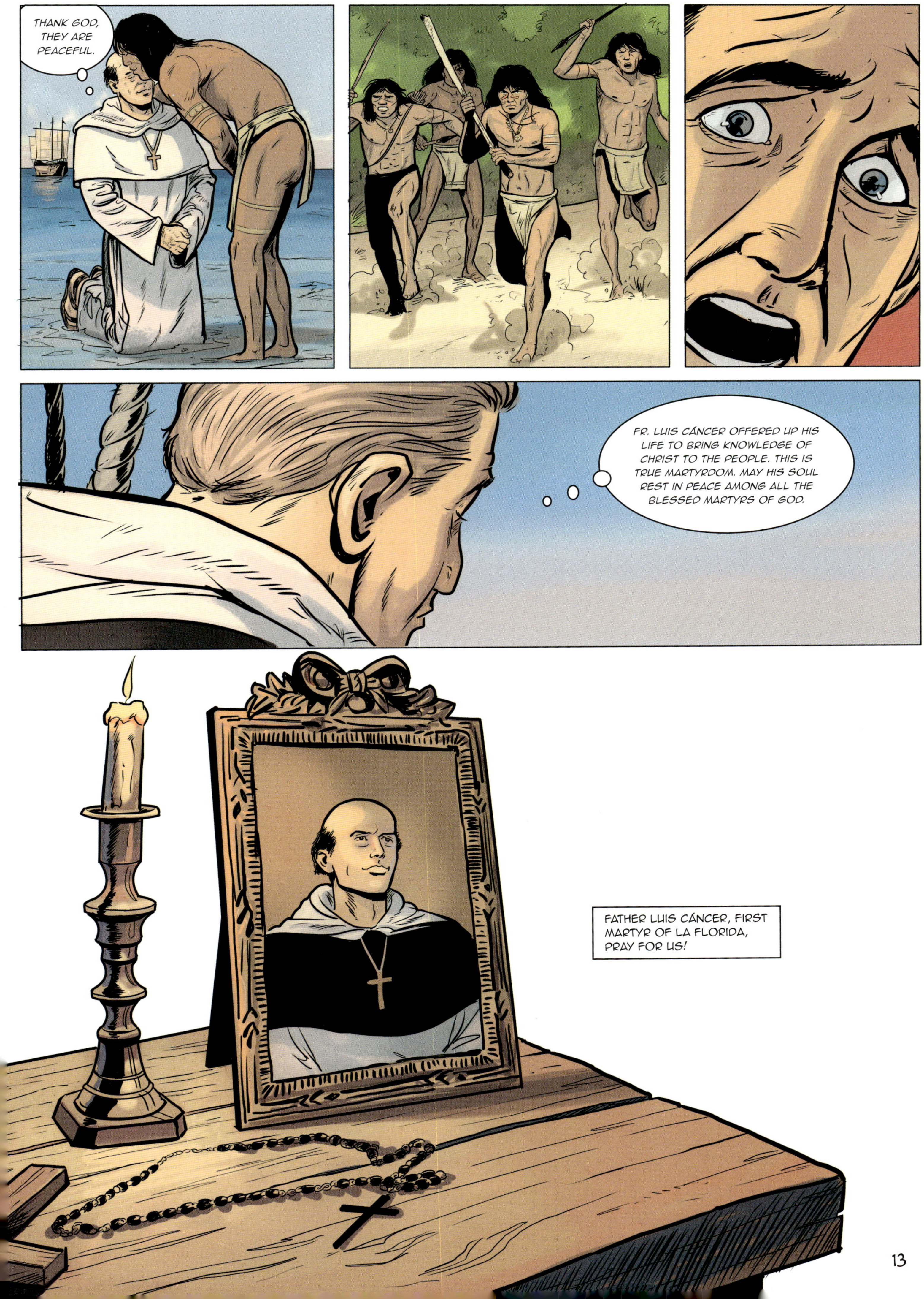
THANK GOD, THEY ARE PEACEFUL.
FR. LUIS CÁNCER OFFERED UP HIS LIFE TO BRING KNOWLEDGE OF CHRIST TO THE PEOPLE. THIS IS TRUE MARTYRDOM. MAY HIS SOUL REST IN PEACE AMONG ALL THE BLESSED MARTYRS OF GOD.
FATHER LUIS CÁNCER, FIRST MARTYR OF LA FLORIDA, PRAY FOR US!

BY 1561, KING PHILIP II OF SPAIN WAS READY TO ABANDON THE COAST OF FLORIDA. THERE HAD BEEN SO MUCH LOSS, AND SO LITTLE PROGRESS. NEARLY FIFTY YEARS AFTER PONCE DE LEÓN SIGHTED THIS LAND, THERE WAS STILL NOT A SINGLE PERMANENT EUROPEAN SETTLEMENT.
BUT PEDRO MENÉNDEZ DE AVILÉS WAS DETERMINED. HE SET FORTH FROM CÁDIZ ON JUNE 29, 1565, WITH NINETEEN SHIPS AND MORE THAN ONE THOUSAND MEN, INCLUDING FOUR PRIESTS (SECULAR PRIESTS, NOT RELIGIOUS).
THREE MONTHS LATER, ON AUGUST 28, THE FEAST OF ST. AUGUSTINE, LAND WAS SIGHTED. FATHER LÓPEZ DESCRIBED THE SCENE...
ON SATURDAY THE 8TH, THE GOVERNOR LANDED WITH MANY BANNERS SPREAD, TO THE SOUND OF TRUMPETS AND SALUTES OF ARTILLERY.
I TOOK A CROSS AND WENT TO MEET HIM, SINGING THE HYMN TE DEUM LAUDAMUS.
THE GOVERNOR, FOLLOWED BY ALL WHO ACCOMPANIED HIM, MARCHED UP TO THE CROSS, KNELT, AND KISSED IT.
A LARGE NUMBER OF INDIANS WATCHED THESE PROCEEDINGS AND IMITATED ALL THEY SAW DONE.
IT WAS SEPTEMBER 8, THE FEAST OF THE NATIVITY OF THE BLESSED VIRGIN MARY. MASS WAS OFFERED IN HER HONOR THAT DAY.
ON THE SITE OF THE FOUNDING OF THE FIRST PARISH, A SHRINE WOULD LATER BE BUILT, IN WHICH THE FATHERS PLACED AN IMAGE OF NUESTRA SEÑORA DE LA LECHE Y BUEN PARTO.
THE PLACE WAS NAMED NOMBRE DE DIOS.
THE IMAGE OF THE BLESSED VIRGIN MARY NURSING THE INFANT JESUS BROUGHT THE GOOD NEWS OF THE INCARNATION TO THE NATIVE PEOPLE.
Your Majesty, if I had a million ducats, I would spend them all on this undertaking in La Florida for the increase of our Holy Catholic Faith...

KINGDOM OF ARAGON (SPAIN).
PEDRO MARTÍNEZ, A BRILLIANT STUDENT AND ATHLETE, JOINED A NEW RELIGIOUS COMMUNITY WHICH WAS BRINGING THE GOSPEL ALL OVER THE WORLD: THE SOCIETY OF JESUS, COMMONLY KNOWN AS THE JESUITS.
I BEG OF YOU, FATHER, LET ME GO TO THE NEW WORLD. LET ME BRING THE NAME OF JESUS TO THOSE WHO HAVE NEVER HEARD IT BEFORE.
THESE MEN HARDLY OPEN THEIR MOUTHS WITHOUT FOUL LANGUAGE, AND THEIR ONLY RECREATION IS DRINKING.
WE ARE MISSIONARIES... WHAT ARE WE WAITING FOR?
WE'LL SING RELIGIOUS SONGS EVERY AFTERNOON... AND LEARN THE CATECHISM. AND FATHER ROGEL AND I WILL BE AVAILABLE FOR CONFESSIONS FOR THE WHOLE CREW.
SOON, THE SHIP WAS QUITE A DIFFERENT PLACE.
FATHER MARTÍNEZ, YOU HAVE TURNED MY SAILORS INTO SAINTS.
FATHER MARTÍNEZ VOLUNTEERED TO GO ASHORE IN SEARCH OF BADLY NEEDED PROVISIONS AND DIRECTIONS, AND SOME FLEMISH SOLDIERS ACCOMPANIED HIM.
DO NOT BE AFRAID, MY BROTHERS. LOOK UPON CHRIST.
FOOD! WE ARE SAVED!
IT APPEARS TO BE A KIND OF GIANT LIZARD.
TRULY, GOD PROVIDED FOR US IN OUR NEED. BUT LET US LEAVE SOMETHING FOR THE PEOPLE IN EXCHANGE FOR THE FOOD WE HAVE EATEN.

FATHER MARTÍNEZ ENCOUNTERED MANY FRIENDLY NATIVES.
THOUGH SOME WELCOMED THEM, OTHERS HAD BEEN TAUGHT BY THE FRENCH HUGUENOTS TO HATE THE SPANISH AND THE CATHOLIC FAITH THEY BROUGHT.
FATHER PEDRO MARTÍNEZ, SJ WAS THE FIRST JESUIT MISSIONARY MARTYR IN NORTH AMERICA.
FATHER PEDRO MARTÍNEZ, MISSIONARY OF THE GOSPEL, PRAY FOR US!
THE JESUITS CONTINUED THEIR EVANGELIZATION WITH RENEWED ZEAL. FATHER JUAN BAUTISTA DE SEGURA, SJ, WAS APPOINTED THE VICE-PROVINCIAL OF FLORIDA.
THUS FAR OUR WORK IN FLORIDA HAS BORN LITTLE FRUIT.
HOW CAN THE FAITH FLOURISH IN THE SHADOW OF THE FORTS? THE INDIANS ARE AFRAID TO COME TO US.
FATHER SEGURA ESTABLISHED A NEW MISSION AT AJACÁN, IN PRESENT-DAY VIRGINIA. THEY BUILT A SIMPLE HOUSE...
AND A CHAPEL...
AND THEY BEGAN TO LIVE LIFE IN COMMUNITY.
WE WILL HAVE TO SUFFER MUCH IF WE ARE TO SUCCEED, BUT I AM HOPEFUL THAT WE WILL BE ABLE TO SERVE OUR LORD AND TO BRING ABOUT MANY CONVERSIONS HERE.
BUT THE MISSION WAS SHORT-LIVED. THEIR NATIVE INTERPRETER ABANDONED THEM. WHEN THEY WENT IN SEARCH OF HIM, THEY WERE ATTACKED.
ALL EIGHT OF THE JESUITS WERE KILLED; ONLY THE YOUNG MAN WHO ASSISTED THE JESUITS SURVIVED TO TELL THE STORY.
FATHER SEGURA AND COMPANIONS, JESUIT MARTYRS OF LA FLORIDA, PRAY FOR US!

DOMINICAN AND JESUIT FATHERS HAD ENCOUNTERED GREAT DIFFICULTIES IN PREACHING THE GOSPEL IN LA FLORIDA, AND MANY HAD GIVEN THEIR LIVES. IN 1574, THE FIRST FRANCISCAN MISSIONARIES ARRIVED. INSPIRED BY ST. FRANCIS OF ASSISI, THEY LIVED IN POVERTY AND SIMPLICITY. FROM GUALE (PRESENT-DAY COASTAL GEORGIA) TO APALACHEE (PRESENT-DAY TALLAHASSEE), THEY LIVED AMONG THE NATIVE PEOPLES.
IN 1604, FATHER MARCOS GARCÉS, OFM, TRAVELED ALL THE WAY FROM ST. AUGUSTINE TO THE APALACHEE PROVINCE.
WE HEARD THAT FRAY PEDRO DE CORPA WAS KILLED SEVEN YEARS AGO BY THE NATIVE PEOPLE UP IN GUALE. DO YOU KNOW WHAT HAPPENED TO HIM, FATHER?
FATHER PEDRO WAS A GOOD MAN. HE USED TO SAY, "IT IS NOT ENOUGH TO BLESS THE PEOPLE, TO PREACH THE WORD. THE SAME HANDS THAT BLESS MUST ALSO PLANT AND BUILD."
MANY OF THE PEOPLE IN GUALE ACCEPTED THE FAITH AND WERE BAPTIZED.
BUT WHEN FATHER DE CORPA TOLD THEM THAT THEY COULD ONLY HAVE ONE WIFE, SOME OF THE MEN BECAME ANGRY. THEY SET UPON FATHER PEDRO AND KILLED HIM, ALONG WITH FOUR OF HIS FRANCISCAN BROTHERS.
O, GOD REWARD THEM! THEY GAVE THEIR LIVES FOR THE HOLY CATHOLIC FAITH!
FATHER MARCOS, WE WISH TO HEAR ABOUT THE GOSPEL, AND ABOUT THE CROSS.
WHILE FATHER MARCOS WAS THERE, THE APALACHEE WERE ATTACKED BY THE TOCOBAGA FROM PRESENT-DAY TAMPA.
THIS IS THE ONE WHO WANTS TO PREVENT US FROM HAVING MORE THAN ONE WIFE.
TAKE OFF THAT GARB YOU WEAR, AND TRAMPLE ON THE CROSS AND YOUR BEADS. THEN WE WILL LET YOU LIVE.
IF YOU WISH TO KILL ME BECAUSE I WEAR THE CROSS, DO IT; I WILL THEN BE WITH GOD IN HEAVEN SOONER THAN I HAD HOPED.
FATHER MARCOS DIED AT THE END OF MAY 1604. HE IS THE PROTO-MARTYR OF TALLAHASSEE.
FATHER MARCOS GARCÉS, COURAGEOUS IN THE FACE OF DEATH, PRAY FOR US!

* PRONOUNCED KAH-SEE-KAY

THE FAITH BEGAN TO FLOURISH.
THE TIMUCUAN PEOPLE HAVE LEARNED TO READ WITH INCREDIBLE RAPIDITY... AFTER ONLY TWO MONTHS' INSTRUCTION, MANY CAN READ AND WRITE LETTERS TO ONE ANOTHER IN THEIR OWN LANGUAGE.
MORE THAN 20,000 OF THE INDIANS HERE HAVE RECEIVED BAPTISM, AND ANOTHER 50,000 HAVE BEEN CATECHIZED.
BUT DO THEY REALLY BELIEVE? OR HAVE THEY ACCEPTED THE CATHOLIC RELIGION BECAUSE IT IS EXPEDIENT FOR THEM TO DO SO?
THEY GO TO MASS AND TO CONFESSION...
THEY SING THE PRAISE OF GOD...
THEY TEACH ONE ANOTHER THE FAITH...
THEY ARE CALLED MARTYRS BECAUSE THEY DIED FOR JESUS CHRIST.
HOW BRAVE THEY WERE!
AND THEY UNDERSTAND THE FAITH BETTER THAN MANY A SPANIARD.
YES, THEY ARE TRUE CHRISTIANS.
MISSION SAN LUIS BECAME THE HEADQUARTERS OF CHRISTIAN APALACHEE. ABOUT 10,000 CHRISTIANS, NATIVES AND SPANISH ALIKE, LIVED NEAR MISSION SAN LUIS. THERE WAS A LARGE CHURCH, A HUGE COUNCIL HOUSE... AND A MILITARY GARRISON.
WE WOULD PREFER NOT TO HAVE THE SOLDIERS SO CLOSE TO OUR MISSION.
WHEN SOME DO NOT BEHAVE LIKE CHRISTIANS, IT GIVES SCANDAL TO THE PEOPLE.

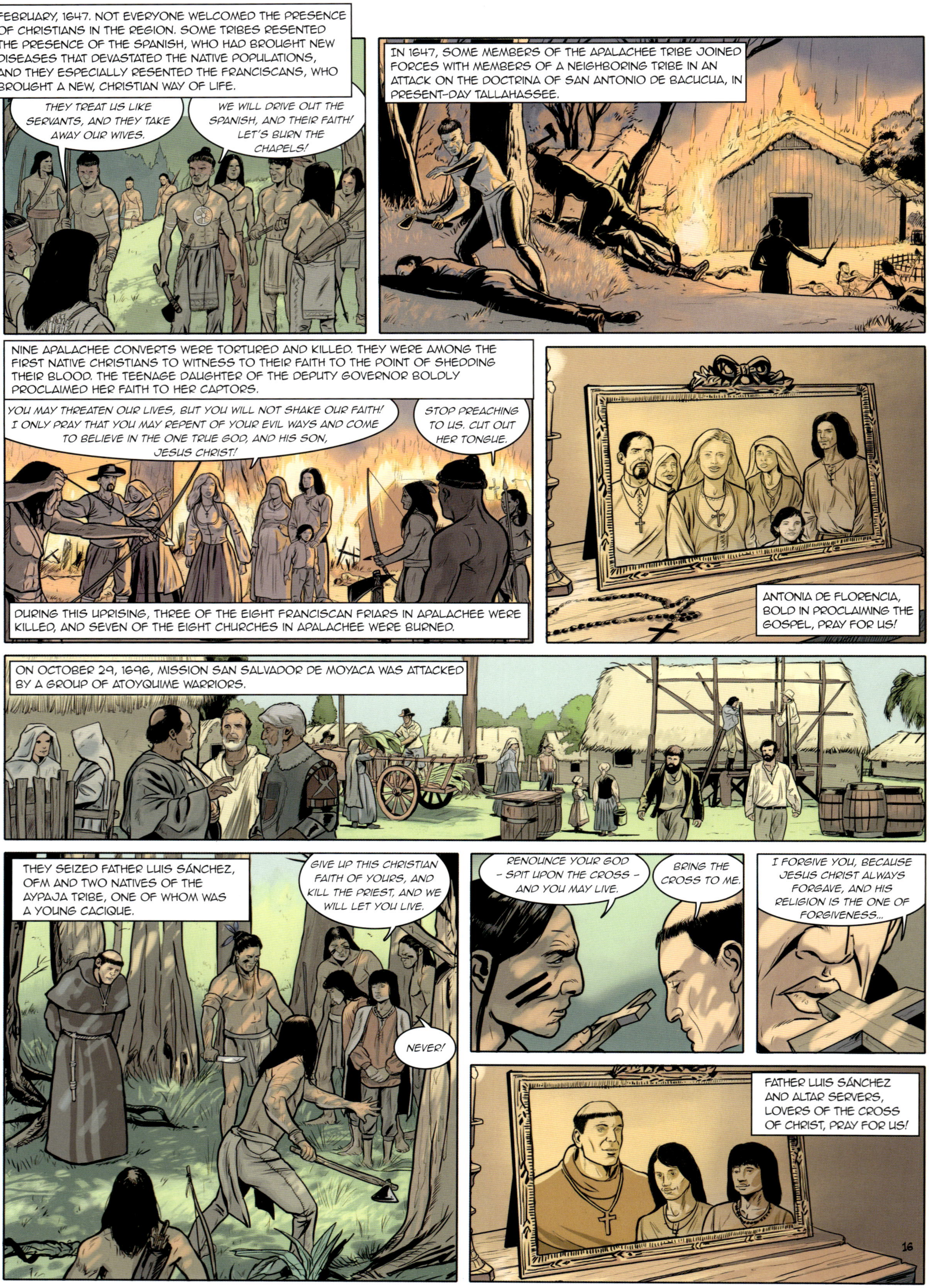
FEBRUARY, 1647. NOT EVERYONE WELCOMED THE PRESENCE OF CHRISTIANS IN THE REGION. SOME TRIBES RESENTED THE PRESENCE OF THE SPANISH, WHO HAD BROUGHT NEW DISEASES THAT DEVASTATED THE NATIVE POPULATIONS, AND THEY ESPECIALLY RESENTED THE FRANCISCANS, WHO BROUGHT A NEW, CHRISTIAN WAY OF LIFE.
THEY TREAT US LIKE SERVANTS, AND THEY TAKE AWAY OUR WIVES.
WE WILL DRIVE OUT THE SPANISH, AND THEIR FAITH! LET'S BURN THE CHAPELS!
IN 1647, SOME MEMBERS OF THE APALACHEE TRIBE JOINED FORCES WITH MEMBERS OF A NEIGHBORING TRIBE IN AN ATTACK ON THE DOCTRINA OF SAN ANTONIO DE BACUCUA, IN PRESENT-DAY TALLAHASSEE.
NINE APALACHEE CONVERTS WERE TORTURED AND KILLED. THEY WERE AMONG THE FIRST NATIVE CHRISTIANS TO WITNESS TO THEIR FAITH TO THE POINT OF SHEDDING THEIR BLOOD. THE TEENAGE DAUGHTER OF THE DEPUTY GOVERNOR BOLDLY PROCLAIMED HER FAITH TO HER CAPTORS.
YOU MAY THREATEN OUR LIVES, BUT YOU WILL NOT SHAKE OUR FAITH! I ONLY PRAY THAT YOU MAY REPENT OF YOUR EVIL WAYS AND COME TO BELIEVE IN THE ONE TRUE GOD, AND HIS SON, JESUS CHRIST!
STOP PREACHING TO US. CUT OUT HER TONGUE.
DURING THIS UPRISING, THREE OF THE EIGHT FRANCISCAN FRIARS IN APALACHEE WERE KILLED, AND SEVEN OF THE EIGHT CHURCHES IN APALACHEE WERE BURNED.
ANTONIA DE FLORENCIA, BOLD IN PROCLAIMING THE GOSPEL, PRAY FOR US!
ON OCTOBER 29, 1696, MISSION SAN SALVADOR DE MOYACA WAS ATTACKED BY A GROUP OF ATOYQUIME WARRIORS.
THEY SEIZED FATHER LUIS SÁNCHEZ, OFM AND TWO NATIVES OF THE AYPAJA TRIBE, ONE OF WHOM WAS A YOUNG CACIQUE.
GIVE UP THIS CHRISTIAN FAITH OF YOURS, AND KILL THE PRIEST, AND WE WILL LET YOU LIVE.
NEVER!
RENOUNCE YOUR GOD - SPIT UPON THE CROSS - AND YOU MAY LIVE.
BRING THE CROSS TO ME.
I FORGIVE YOU, BECAUSE JESUS CHRIST ALWAYS FORGAVE, AND HIS RELIGION IS THE ONE OF FORGIVENESS...
FATHER LUIS SÁNCHEZ AND ALTAR SERVERS, LOVERS OF THE CROSS OF CHRIST, PRAY FOR US!
16

THE FAITH SURVIVED AND FLOURISHED IN APALACHEE, WHERE THE PEOPLE REBUILT THEIR CHURCHES.
IN 1674, BISHOP GABRIEL DÍAZ VARA CALDERÓN OF SANTIAGO DE CUBA VISITED THE MISSIONS. HE CONFIRMED 13,152 CHRISTIAN CONVERTS!
THERE MUST BE 3,000 PEOPLE HERE! WHAT AN EXTRAORDINARY BUILDING.
THIS IS TRULY A WISE AND REMARKABLE PEOPLE. THEIR FAITH AND DEVOTION SEEM TO KNOW NO BOUNDS. I WILL SEND MORE FRIARS TO APALACHEE TO ASSIST IN THIS HOLY WORK. BUT PLEASE, FATHER - DO WHAT YOU CAN TO DISCOURAGE THIS DANGEROUS AND SUPERSTITIOUS GAME OF BALL!
BISHOP CALDERÓN WROTE TO QUEEN MARIANA TO DESCRIBE WHAT HE HAD SEEN.
They embrace with devotion the mysteries of our holy Faith... They are very devoted to the Virgin, and on Saturdays they attend when her Mass is sung.
17

THE ENGLISH WERE MOVING FURTHER AND FURTHER SOUTH. IN 1670, THEY ESTABLISHED A NEW SETTLEMENT WHICH THEY NAMED "CHARLES TOWN."
WE NEED TO DRIVE OUT THE CATHOLICS WHO TEACH THE INDIANS THEY ARE EQUAL TO US.
THE ENGLISH ESTABLISHED ALLIANCES WITH THE CREEK AND YAMASEE INDIANS AND BEGAN CONDUCTING RAIDS ON APALACHEE VILLAGES, KIDNAPPING MEN, WOMEN AND CHILDREN WHOM THEY SOLD AS SLAVES.
THE APALACHEE WERE DETERMINED TO FIGHT BACK.
WE HAVE NO PEACE WHILE THESE RAIDERS ARE KILLING OUR FAMILIES AND TAKING OUR YOUNG WOMEN.
GO, THEN, AND MAY GOD GO WITH YOU.
THIS TIME THE APALACHEE WERE SUCCESSFUL... BUT THE ENGLISH AND THEIR ALLIES WOULD RETURN AGAIN AND AGAIN.
NOVEMBER, 1702.
WE HAVE TO DRIVE OUT OUR ENEMIES. LET US DESTROY THE CATHOLIC MISSIONS - THEY ARE THE SOURCE OF SPANISH STRENGTH IN THIS REGION.
WE CAN TAKE MANY SLAVES, AND GROW RICH!
LET US COMMENCE OUR ATTACK ON ST. AUGUSTINE.
18

THE ENGLISH ARE ABOUT TO ATTACK. OH, TAKE CARE, OR MANY LIVES WILL BE LOST!
IF WE DESTROY THE FAITH, WE DESTROY THE PEOPLE.
ST. AUGUSTINE ITSELF WAS RAZED TO THE GROUND... THE CHAPEL OF NUESTRA SEÑORA DE LA LECHE WAS BURNED, AND THE LIBRARY OF THE FRIARS WAS DESTROYED.
EVEN THE HOLY BIBLE ITSELF WAS NOT SPARED, BECAUSE THE TEXT WAS IN LATIN.
BUT THE CASTILLO DE SAN MARCOS STOOD FIRM AGAINST THE ATTACK. THE ENGLISH WERE FORCED TO WITHDRAW.
JUST BEFORE THE SIEGE OF CASTILLO SAN MARCOS, CREEK ALLIES OF THE ENGLISH ATTACKED THE MISSION OF SAN JUAN DEL PUERTO, A TIMUCUAN CHRISTIAN VILLAGE. MOST OF THE FORTY TIMUCUAN PEOPLE LIVING THERE WERE KILLED BECAUSE THEY WOULD NOT SPIT ON THE CROSS.
MARIANA WAS THE WIDOWED DAUGHTER OF THE CACIQUE, AND HER SON JACINTO, WAS JUST NINE YEARS OLD.
YOU ARE THE DAUGHTER OF A CHIEF. RENOUNCE YOUR CATHOLIC RELIGION AND SPIT UPON THE CROSS.
I WOULD JUST AS SOON TEAR OUT MY HEART – FOR THE CROSS AND MY HEART ARE ONE AND THE SAME.
THEN YOU MUST DIE, BUT FIRST, WE WILL KILL YOUR SON.
HAIL MARY, FULL OF GRACE, THE LORD IS WITH THEE...
ALL THROUGH THEIR LAST AGONY, THEY PRAYED THE ROSARY TOGETHER.
HOLY MARY, MOTHER OF GOD, PRAY FOR US SINNERS...
...NOW AND AT THE HOUR OF OUR DEATH. AMEN.
MARIANA AND JACINTO, FAITHFUL TO THE END, PRAY FOR US!

MEANWHILE, AT MISSION SAN LUIS...
THE APALACHEE PEOPLE LIVING IN AND AROUND MISSION SAN LUIS HAD AN EXTRAORDINARY LEADER IN ANTONIO CUIPA. ANTONIO WAS THE SON OF CHRISTIAN APALACHEES, BORN AND RAISED AT MISSION SAN LUIS. HE WAS THE *INIJA*, THE SECOND-IN-COMMAND.
SAINT JOSEPH, YOU WERE A CARPENTER, A HUSBAND, AND A FATHER, LIKE ME. HELP ME TO BE WISE AND PRUDENT LIKE YOU. PLEASE HELP MY APALACHEE PEOPLE TO BE ONE, SINGLE, HOLY FAMILY – LIKE YOURS. HELP ME TO KEEP THEM SAFE.
ANTONIO COULD READ AND WRITE IN LATIN AND SPANISH, AND HE OFTEN ACCOMPANIED THE FRANCISCANS ON THEIR MISSIONARY JOURNEYS. HE ALSO WENT ON MISSIONARY JOURNEYS WITH OTHER CHRISTIAN NATIVES, EVEN, AT TIMES, WITHOUT THE FRIARS.
ANTONIO'S PREACHING TOUCHES THEIR HEARTS IN A WAY OURS DOES NOT.
HE IS ALWAYS GENTLE; HE LISTENS AS WELL AS SPEAKS. HE IS A TRUE EVANGELIST.
DETERMINED TO RESTORE HIS REPUTATION AFTER HIS FAILURE TO TAKE CASTILLO SAN MARCOS, JAMES MOORE RECRUITED FIFTY ENGLISH AND MORE THAN 1,000 CREEKS TO DESTROY THE FLORIDA MISSIONS ONCE AND FOR ALL.
JANUARY 25, 1704. MOORE AND HIS FORCES ATTACKED THE MISSION OF LA CONCEPCIÓN DE AYUBALE.
CACIQUE! THE ENGLISH ARE AT AYUBALE! IF WE DON'T HELP THEM, THE PEOPLE AND MISSION WILL BE LOST!
I MUST GO, JOSEFA. FOR YOU, FOR THEM, FOR ALL OUR PEOPLE. FOR THE HOLY CATHOLIC FAITH.
GO, MY LOVE, AND MAY GOD GO WITH YOU.
ANTONIO WAS READY. A FEW MONTHS BEFORE, HE HAD WRITTEN HIS LAST WILL AND TESTAMENT...
"...Fearing as I do that the hour
of my death may come in these times that are times of
war and of attacks from the enemies, and believing as
do, firmly and faithfully, in the Holy Mystery of
Most Holy Trinity, I want to die as a Catholic and
Christian... I am bequeathing to the Indian Josefa, my
wife, a Catechism book and the Crucifix that was a
from Father Méndez, as well as the medals of
and my prayer beads...
TODAY WILL BE A DAY OF GREAT GLORY. YOU WILL DIE DEFENDING THE LAW OF GOD. I WILL GO WITH YOU FOR YOUR ENCOURAGEMENT, READY TO DIE WITH MY CHILDREN.
THE CHRISTIAN WARRIORS OF MISSION SAN LUIS AND AYUBALE FOUGHT BRAVELY, BUT THEY WERE VASTLY OUTNUMBERED. MANY WERE KILLED. ANTONIO WAS CAPTURED.

I AM HAPPY TO DIE IN THIS WAY, AS MY MASTER DIED.
DO YOU SEE WHAT THEY ARE DOING? YOU CALL YOURSELF A CHRISTIAN – PUT A STOP TO THIS, I BEG OF YOU.
IT IS THE CUSTOM OF THE CREEKS. I CAN DO NOTHING.
IF YOU, THEIR LEADER, WILL DO NOTHING, THEN I WILL GO TO THEIR AID.
MAKE MORE FIRE SO THAT OUR HEARTS MAY BE ALLOWED TO SUFFER FOR OUR SOULS. WE GO TO ENJOY GOD AS CHRISTIANS.
LORD, HAVE MERCY. LORD, HAVE MERCY.
I SEE OUR LADY! I AM LOOKING INTO HER EYES! SHE IS GIVING ME THE STRENGTH TO ENDURE THIS MARTYRDOM.
ANTONIO CUIPA DIED ON JANUARY 26, 1704.
WHAT DOES HE SEE? I SEE NOTHING.
MY BODY WILL FALL TO THE GROUND. MY SOUL IS GOING TO GOD.
ANTONIO, FAITHFUL HUSBAND AND FATHER, EVANGELIST, TEACHER, LEADER, AND MARTYR FOR CHRIST, PRAY FOR US!

* A FEMALE CHIEF.

A NEW DOCTRINA IN THE APALACHEE PROVINCE WAS MARY IMMACULATE, IN PRESENT-DAY JEFFERSON COUNTY.
FATHER, WHEN THE MISSION IS BLESSED, MAY I SERVE AT THE ALTAR?
YES, MANUEL. WHO KNOWS, PERHAPS ONE DAY YOU MAY BECOME A PRIEST.
OH, FATHER, I WOULD BE SO HONORED TO SERVE GOD ALL DAY LONG LIKE YOU AND THE FRIARS!
EARLY IN 1704, THE ENGLISH AND CREEKS ATTACKED THE NEW MISSION, BURNING IT TO THE GROUND. THE NEW CHURCH WAS SET ON FIRE.
RUN, MANUEL! RUN!
HELP, HELP! GOD'S HOUSE IS ON FIRE!
IF YOUR GOD IS SO POWERFUL, LET HIM MAKE IT RAIN SO THAT THE FIRE MAY BE EXTINGUISHED WITH WATER FROM HEAVEN.
THIS IS THE HOUSE OF GOD! WE MUST PUT OUT THE FIRE!
SILENCE THAT BOY.
MANUEL KEPT PRAYING ALOUD. THE WARRIORS CUT OFF HIS ARMS TO KEEP HIM FROM RAISING THEM TO GOD, AND THEN DROWNED HIM IN THE WATERING TROUGH FOR ANIMALS.
MANUEL, DEFENDER OF THE HOUSE OF GOD, PRAY FOR US!

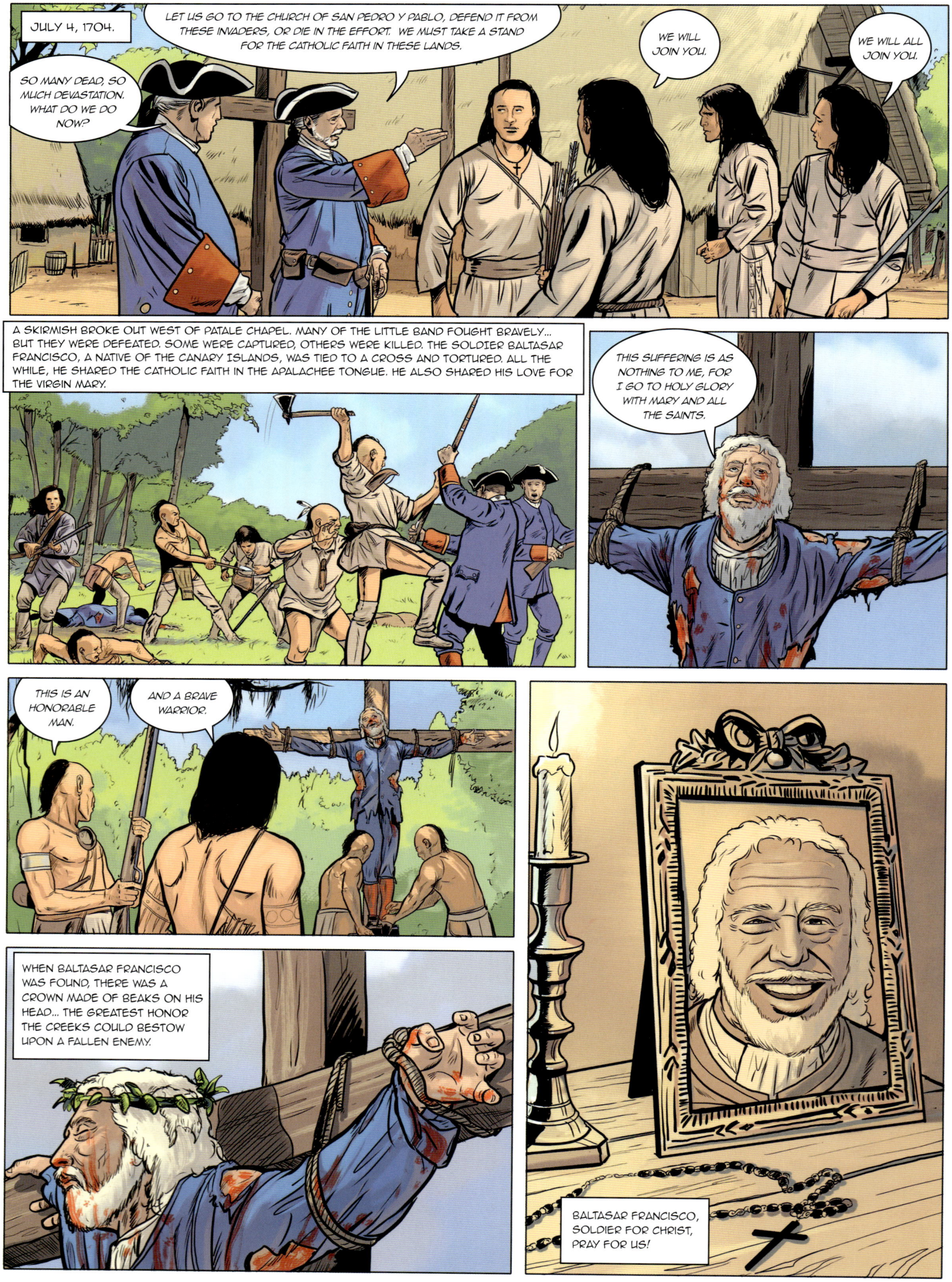
JULY 4, 1704.
SO MANY DEAD, SO MUCH DEVASTATION. WHAT DO WE DO NOW?
LET US GO TO THE CHURCH OF SAN PEDRO Y PABLO, DEFEND IT FROM THESE INVADERS, OR DIE IN THE EFFORT. WE MUST TAKE A STAND FOR THE CATHOLIC FAITH IN THESE LANDS.
WE WILL JOIN YOU.
WE WILL ALL JOIN YOU.
A SKIRMISH BROKE OUT WEST OF PATALE CHAPEL. MANY OF THE LITTLE BAND FOUGHT BRAVELY... BUT THEY WERE DEFEATED. SOME WERE CAPTURED, OTHERS WERE KILLED. THE SOLDIER BALTASAR FRANCISCO, A NATIVE OF THE CANARY ISLANDS, WAS TIED TO A CROSS AND TORTURED. ALL THE WHILE, HE SHARED THE CATHOLIC FAITH IN THE APALACHEE TONGUE. HE ALSO SHARED HIS LOVE FOR THE VIRGIN MARY.
THIS SUFFERING IS AS NOTHING TO ME, FOR I GO TO HOLY GLORY WITH MARY AND ALL THE SAINTS.
THIS IS AN HONORABLE MAN.
AND A BRAVE WARRIOR.
WHEN BALTASAR FRANCISCO WAS FOUND, THERE WAS A CROWN MADE OF BEAKS ON HIS HEAD... THE GREATEST HONOR THE CREEKS COULD BESTOW UPON A FALLEN ENEMY.
BALTASAR FRANCISCO, SOLDIER FOR CHRIST, PRAY FOR US!

IT WAS THE LAST STAND FOR CATHOLIC APALACHEE... THOUSANDS OF CHRISTIAN INDIANS HAD BEEN KILLED OR ENSLAVED. SOME OF THE SURVIVORS WENT WEST TO ALABAMA AND EVENTUALLY TO LOUISIANA. OTHERS STAYED WITH THE SPANISH AND WALKED EL CAMINO REAL TO ST. AUGUSTINE, HEARTBROKEN, LEAVING THEIR HOMELAND FOREVER. THE APALACHEE BROUGHT THEIR FAITH WITH THEM. EVEN AMONG THE CAPTIVES IN CHARLESTON, THE APALACHEE CACIQUES CIRILO AND PEDRO AND AN APALACHEE MAN NAMED VICTOR WERE KILLED WHEN THEY REFUSED TO RENOUNCE THEIR FAITH.
THE SPLENDID CHAIN OF MISSIONS WOULD NEVER BE REBUILT.
WHERE ARE YOU GOING, FATHER CRIADO? COME TO ST. AUGUSTINE WHERE IT IS SAFE. THERE IS NOTHING LEFT OF APALACHEE.
I HAVE HEARD OF A FEW CHRISTIAN INDIANS WHO ARE STILL HERE IN HIDING. I WILL FIND THEM AND MINISTER TO THEM.
EVENTUALLY FATHER CRIADO SHARED THE FATE OF SO MANY OF THE CHRISTIAN APALACHEE PEOPLE: HE WAS CAPTURED AND KEPT AS A SLAVE.
FATHER TIBURCIO! YOU'RE ALIVE! WE WERE TOLD YOU HAD BEEN KILLED AT MISSION SAN LUIS. THANKS BE TO GOD! WHAT HAPPENED, FATHER? TELL ME.
FATHER CRIADO! I ONLY CAN SPEAK OF THE SUFFERING OF MY LORD, PILATE TOOK JESUS AND HAD HIM SCOURGED. AND THE SOLDIERS WOVE A CROWN OUT OF THORNS AND PLACED IT ON HIS HEAD...
IN NOMINE PATRIS, ET FILII, ET SPIRITUS SANCTI...
FATHER TIBURCIO WAS EVENTUALLY RELEASED AND SENT TO ST. AUGUSTINE WHERE HE DIED AS A RESULT OF THE TORTURES HE HAD ENDURED. FATHER CRIADO ALSO DIED AS A RESULT OF HIS TREATMENT IN CAPTIVITY.
FATHER CRIADO AND FATHER TIBURCIO, PRIESTS AND SERVANTS OF THE LORD, PRAY FOR US!

SEPTEMBER 3, 1705. THE MASSACRE OF THE APALACHEE WAS OVER, BUT BRITISH AND CREEKS CONTINUED TO HARASS THE SPANISH AND THE NATIVE CHRISTIANS OF MANY TRIBES LIVING OUTSIDE ST. AUGUSTINE.
FATHER, THEY HAVE RAIDED THE MISSION – THEY HAVE TAKEN JACINTO AND JULIO.
THEY ARE ONLY CHILDREN!
WE HAVE NO WEAPONS, WE COME IN PEACE.
THEY ARE JUST BOYS! FOR THE LOVE OF GOD, LET THEM GO. TAKE ME INSTEAD.
FATHER AGUSTÍN PONCE DE LEÓN, BORN IN ST. AUGUSTINE, WAS THE FIRST NATIVE-BORN PRIEST AND MARTYR OF WHAT WOULD BECOME THE UNITED STATES.
JACINTO, JULIO, AND FATHER AGUSTÍN, FAITHFUL UNTO DEATH, PRAY FOR US!
SANTA MARÍA DE GALVE (PRESENT-DAY PENSACOLA).
THEY ARE COMING, FATHER LUCIO!
WE MUST SAVE THE BLESSED SACRAMENT IF WE CAN.
YES! RUN! LEAVE ME!
AAH!!!
FATHER PEDRO AND FATHER LUCIO, MARTYRS OF THE EUCHARIST, PRAY FOR US!

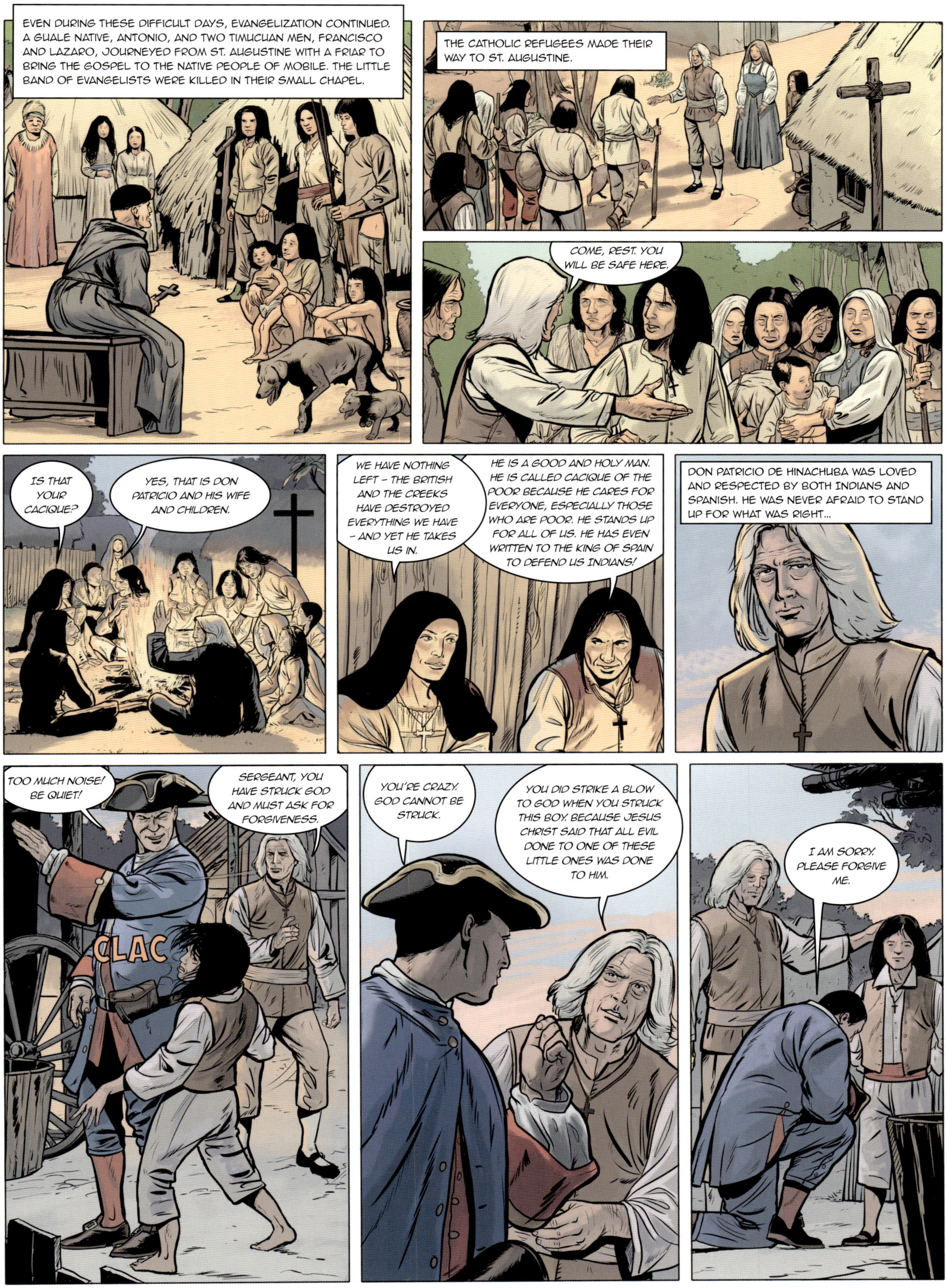

EVEN DURING THESE DIFFICULT DAYS, EVANGELIZATION CONTINUED. A GUALE NATIVE, ANTONIO, AND TWO TIMUCUAN MEN, FRANCISCO AND LAZARO, JOURNEYED FROM ST. AUGUSTINE WITH A FRIAR TO BRING THE GOSPEL TO THE NATIVE PEOPLE OF MOBILE. THE LITTLE BAND OF EVANGELISTS WERE KILLED IN THEIR SMALL CHAPEL.
THE CATHOLIC REFUGEES MADE THEIR WAY TO ST. AUGUSTINE.
COME, REST. YOU WILL BE SAFE HERE.
IS THAT YOUR CACIQUE?
YES, THAT IS DON PATRICIO AND HIS WIFE AND CHILDREN.
WE HAVE NOTHING LEFT – THE BRITISH AND THE CREEKS HAVE DESTROYED EVERYTHING WE HAVE – AND YET HE TAKES US IN.
HE IS A GOOD AND HOLY MAN. HE IS CALLED CACIQUE OF THE POOR BECAUSE HE CARES FOR EVERYONE, ESPECIALLY THOSE WHO ARE POOR. HE STANDS UP FOR ALL OF US. HE HAS EVEN WRITTEN TO THE KING OF SPAIN TO DEFEND US INDIANS!
DON PATRICIO DE HINACHUBA WAS LOVED AND RESPECTED BY BOTH INDIANS AND SPANISH. HE WAS NEVER AFRAID TO STAND UP FOR WHAT WAS RIGHT...
TOO MUCH NOISE! BE QUIET!
CLAC
SERGEANT, YOU HAVE STRUCK GOD AND MUST ASK FOR FORGIVENESS.
YOU'RE CRAZY. GOD CANNOT BE STRUCK.
YOU DID STRIKE A BLOW TO GOD WHEN YOU STRUCK THIS BOY. BECAUSE JESUS CHRIST SAID THAT ALL EVIL DONE TO ONE OF THESE LITTLE ONES WAS DONE TO HIM.
I AM SORRY. PLEASE FORGIVE ME.

DON PATRICIO AND HIS COMMUNITY LIVED UNDER CONSTANT THREAT OF ATTACK. BUT THEY KEPT THE FAITH AND WERE JOYFUL.
BUT THE ENGLISH-DRIVEN ATTACKS CONTINUED RELENTLESSLY.
SPIT UPON THIS CROSS, AND YOU SHALL LIVE. IF NOT, YOU SHALL SUFFER AS NO ONE HAS EVER SUFFERED BEFORE.
FOR A SHORT WHILE I MAY SUFFER PAIN AND DEATH, BUT THEN COMES LIFE ETERNAL WITH GOD IN HEAVEN. THEREFORE I AM NOT AFRAID. MAKE HASTE, THEN, THAT I MAY SOON BE TOGETHER WITH MY GOD AND LORD.
DON PATRICIO, PEACEMAKER AND LEADER, PRAY FOR US!

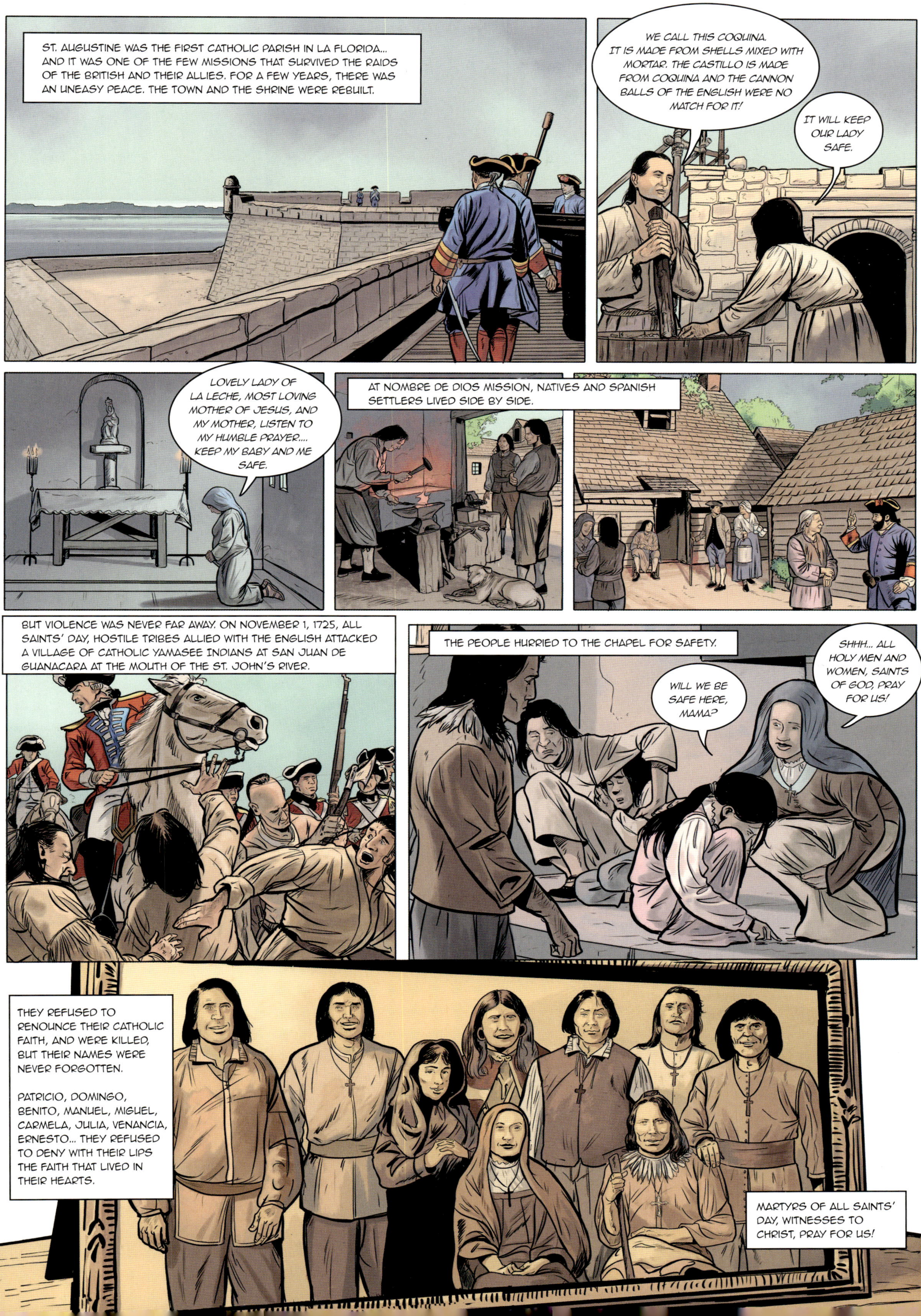

ST. AUGUSTINE WAS THE FIRST CATHOLIC PARISH IN LA FLORIDA... AND IT WAS ONE OF THE FEW MISSIONS THAT SURVIVED THE RAIDS OF THE BRITISH AND THEIR ALLIES. FOR A FEW YEARS, THERE WAS AN UNEASY PEACE. THE TOWN AND THE SHRINE WERE REBUILT.
WE CALL THIS COQUINA. IT IS MADE FROM SHELLS MIXED WITH MORTAR. THE CASTILLO IS MADE FROM COQUINA AND THE CANNON BALLS OF THE ENGLISH WERE NO MATCH FOR IT!
IT WILL KEEP OUR LADY SAFE.
LOVELY LADY OF LA LECHE, MOST LOVING MOTHER OF JESUS, AND MY MOTHER, LISTEN TO MY HUMBLE PRAYER.... KEEP MY BABY AND ME SAFE.
AT NOMBRE DE DIOS MISSION, NATIVES AND SPANISH SETTLERS LIVED SIDE BY SIDE.
BUT VIOLENCE WAS NEVER FAR AWAY. ON NOVEMBER 1, 1725, ALL SAINTS' DAY, HOSTILE TRIBES ALLIED WITH THE ENGLISH ATTACKED A VILLAGE OF CATHOLIC YAMASEE INDIANS AT SAN JUAN DE GUANACARA AT THE MOUTH OF THE ST. JOHN'S RIVER.
THE PEOPLE HURRIED TO THE CHAPEL FOR SAFETY.
WILL WE BE SAFE HERE, MAMA?
SHHH... ALL HOLY MEN AND WOMEN, SAINTS OF GOD, PRAY FOR US!
THEY REFUSED TO RENOUNCE THEIR CATHOLIC FAITH, AND WERE KILLED, BUT THEIR NAMES WERE NEVER FORGOTTEN.
PATRICIO, DOMINGO, BENITO, MANUEL, MIGUEL, CARMELA, JULIA, VENANCIA, ERNESTO... THEY REFUSED TO DENY WITH THEIR LIPS THE FAITH THAT LIVED IN THEIR HEARTS.
MARTYRS OF ALL SAINTS' DAY, WITNESSES TO CHRIST, PRAY FOR US!

COLONEL JOHN PALMER OF SOUTH CAROLINA WAS DETERMINED TO DRIVE THE SPANISH OUT OF FLORIDA. ON DECEMBER 16, 1727, HE RAIDED NOMBRE DE DIOS CHIQUITO, A SMALL SETTLEMENT NOT FAR FROM ST. AUGUSTINE.
JOSEPH WAS A TRANSLATOR. TOO THIN AND WEAK TO BE A WARRIOR, HE SPENT HIS LIFE IN SERVICE OF THE NEEDS OF THE CHURCH, TEACHING CATECHISM, TRANSLATING FOR THE FRIARS, TENDING TO THE CHAPEL OF OUR LADY OF LA LECHE.
JESUS, PLEASE ACCEPT MY SMALL SERVICE AS A PRAYER...I LOVE YOU.
LOOK! THEY WERE GOING TO DESTROY THE CHAPEL SO JOSEPH TOOK THE PRECIOUS BODY OF THE LORD AWAY.
HE HAS DIED A MARTYR FOR HIS LORD AND GOD.
JOSEPH, SACRISTAN AND HOLY WITNESS TO THE EUCHARIST, PRAY FOR US!

IN 1739, GOVERNOR JAMES OGLETHORPE, THE ENGLISH FOUNDER OF THE COLONY OF GEORGIA, SET HIS SIGHTS ON ST. AUGUSTINE. HE INVADED IN SEPTEMBER 1739, BUT HIS FORCES WERE TURNED BACK BY CATHOLIC YBAJA INDIANS, LED BY THEIR CACIQUES, JUAN IGNACIO DE LOS REYES AND BAUTISTA DEL NIÑO JESÚS.
YOU ARE THE CACIQUE, ARE YOU? RENOUNCE THIS CATHOLIC FAITH OF YOURS, OR DIE.
I WILL NOT. I FORGIVE YOU, FOR YOU DO NOT KNOW WHAT YOU ARE DOING.
BAUTISTA WAS BURIED UNDER THE ALTAR OF THE VILLAGE CHURCH.
WHAT NAME HAVE YOU GIVEN TO YOUR CHILD?
BAUTISTA! WE WISH OUR CHILDREN TO HAVE THE SAME FAITH AS BAUTISTA.
EVERY CHILD IN THIS VILLAGE IS CALLED BAUTISTA! IT IS WONDERFUL THAT YOU WISH TO HONOR OUR BLESSED MARTYR BAUTISTA. BUT PLEASE, CALL THEM BY SOME OTHER NAME!
BAUTISTA, BELOVED CACIQUE AND MARTYR, PRAY FOR US!
IN JUNE 1740, OGLETHORPE RENEWED THE SIEGE OF ST. AUGUSTINE, THIS TIME FROM THE SEA. RAIDING PARTIES SKIRMISHED ON SHORE. ON JULY 22, 1740, THEY ATTACKED THE SHRINE OF OUR LADY OF LA LECHE AGAIN... BUT IT WAS NOT WITHOUT DEFENDERS.
YOU MUST NOT DESTROY THIS PLACE, FOR IT IS THE HOUSE OF GOD!
GET OUT OF THE WAY!
WE WILL NOT ABANDON OUR LADY.
EVENTUALLY THE ENGLISH WERE PUSHED BACK... BUT ELADIO AND ROBERTO WERE FOUND DEAD BEFORE THE ALTAR.
ELADIO AND ROBERTO, FEARLESS DEFENDERS OF OUR LADY OF LA LECHE, PRAY FOR US!
THE BRITISH BOMBARDMENT OF ST. AUGUSTINE LASTED 27 DAYS. ULTIMATELY IT FAILED AND OGLETHORPE AND HIS TROOPS WERE FORCED TO RETREAT.

CATHOLIC FLORIDA WAS BROKEN AND SCATTERED BY VIOLENCE AND HATRED, BUT SMALL COMMUNITIES OF NATIVES CONTINUED TO PRACTICE THEIR FAITH.
IN PENSACOLA, NEAR THE SEA, WAS A SMALL CHRISTIAN COMMUNITY OF CHICASA INDIANS. AMONG THEM WAS ANTONIO, WHO WAS CALLED "THE BLESSED INDIAN" OR "ANTONIO BENDITO," "ANTONIO THE BLESSED," BECAUSE OF HIS HOLY LIFE AND GENEROSITY.
HE SHARED WHAT HE HAD WITH THOSE WHO HAD NOTHING.
HE ASSISTED AT MASS AND HELPED THE FRANCISCANS TO TEACH THE FAITH.
WHEN THE RAIDERS CAME, ANTONIO BENDITO, WHO WAS FISHING ALONG WITH OTHER MEMBERS OF HIS TRIBE, REFUSED TO BE TAKEN AWAY.
REPENT OF WHAT YOU ARE DOING, FREE THESE PEOPLE, AND ASK GOD'S FORGIVENESS. I WILL NOT GO WITH YOU. AS FOR ME, I THINK IT IS BETTER TO DIE HERE, A FREE AND FAITHFUL CATHOLIC, THAN TO RENOUNCE MY FAITH AND LIVE AS A SLAVE.
ANTONIO AND SEVERAL OTHERS WERE BEATEN, THEN BURNED.
IT WAS MARCH 22, 1760.
ANTONIO THE BLESSED, SERVANT OF THE POOR, PRAY FOR US!
BRITISH FORCES CONTINUED TO CONDUCT RAIDS ON THE SURVIVING CATHOLIC COMMUNITIES NEAR PENSACOLA BAY.
QUICK! TO THE CHAPEL! WE MUST PROTECT THE BLESSED SACRAMENT.
ELPIDIO JOSE, ALBERTO, AND MATIAS EL CHICO, LOVERS OF THE EUCHARIST, PRAY FOR US!
THEY WERE THE LAST OF THE FLORIDA MARTYRS.
IN 1763 THE REMAINING APALACHEE PEOPLE WERE DRIVEN FROM FLORIDA, BUT A REMNANT SURVIVED.
SOME FLORIDA CATHOLIC NATIVES HEADED WEST, WHILE OTHERS WENT WITH THE SPANISH TO HAVANA.
THE ONCE FLOURISHING FLORIDA MISSIONS VANISHED, ALMOST WITHOUT A TRACE.

BUT THE PEOPLE OF LA FLORIDA NEVER FORGOT THEIR MARTYRS. THEIR CONTEMPORARIES AND THE GENERATIONS THAT FOLLOWED REMEMBERED THEM AND TOLD THEIR STORIES.
THEY WERE HONORED BY POPES AND KINGS.
1743.
BY THE POWER GRANTED ME BY THE HOLY SEE, I, PHILIP V OF SPAIN, DECREE THAT ON OCTOBER 3 SHALL BE COMMEMORATED YEARLY THE MARTYRS OF LA FLORIDA.
FLORIDA'S FIRST RESIDENT BISHOP, BISHOP AUGUSTIN VEROT, WAS DEVOTED TO THE FLORIDA MARTYRS.
FLORIDA HAS BEEN BEDEWED IN THE EAST AND THE WEST, IN THE NORTH AND IN THE SOUTH WITH THE PUREST BLOOD OF MARTYRS!
IN THE 19TH CENTURY, THE HISTORY OF THE FLORIDA MARTYRS BEGAN TO BE RECOVERED AND CELEBRATED. DEVOTION TO OUR LADY OF LA LECHE CONTINUED TO GROW.
IN 1939, BISHOP JOHN MARK GANNON OF ERIE TOOK UP THE CAUSE OF THE MARTYRS.
WHY SOMETHING HAS NOT BEEN DONE IN THIS MATTER BEFORE, IS A MYSTERY TO ME. I AM FASCINATED WITH IT ALL.
BISHOP GANNON APPOINTED A GROUP OF SCHOLARS. 1941.
REV. ROLAND BURKE, OFM; REV. MICHAEL KENNY, SJ; MOST REV. JOHN MARK GANNON, DD; REV. JOHN WYNNE, SJ; REV. MARION HABIG, OFM; REV. JAMES POWERS, MA.
THE CHRISTIAN SEED PLANTED BY THE CATHOLIC MARTYRS, TILLED AND WATERED BY THE CATHOLIC PIETY OF MILLIONS OF IMMIGRANTS, HAS MATURED INTO A GREAT NATION. WE ARE THE LEGITIMATE AND PROUD DESCENDANTS OF THE EARLY MARTYRS OF THE UNITED STATES.

THIS CAUSE IS BEAUTIFUL... MOST BEAUTIFUL.
I am afraid the war has cut across our intent to secure canonization for the martyrs of America. Nevertheless, our labor has not been in vain.... If the result doesn't come while we are still on earth, there may be added joy and interest in watching the mortals work out an answer to the problem from the blissful skies above.
Bishop John Mark Gannon
1944
IN 1982, BISHOP RENÉ HENRY GRACIDA, THE FIRST BISHOP OF PENSACOLA-TALLAHASSEE, TOOK UP THE CAUSE ONCE MORE.
THE MARTYRS SHOULD HAVE A PLACE IN OUR RELIGIOUS MEMORIES, SO THAT THEIR LIVES MIGHT INSPIRE AND TEACH THAT SERVICE INVOLVES SACRIFICE.
IN 2005, LAY PEOPLE IN TALLAHASSEE RENEWED THE DEVOTION TO THE FLORIDA MARTYRS AND IT SPREAD.
LAY PEOPLE PETITIONED THE VATICAN.
PRIESTS AND LAY PEOPLE WERE COMMISSIONED TO PURSUE THE MARTYRS' BEATIFICATION.
BISHOP WILLIAM WACK, CSC., OF PENSACOLA-TALLAHASSEE LEADS THE CAUSE.
POSTULATORS IN ROME SHEPHERD THE CAUSE.
HISTORIANS STUDY THE MARTYRS' STORIES.
THE CAUSE COMES BEFORE A TRIBUNAL OF CANON LAWYERS.

FOR HUNDREDS OF YEARS, THE FAITHFUL OF *LA FLORIDA* GAVE THEIR LIVES TO DEFEND THE PRESENCE OF THE EUCHARIST IN THEIR LAND. ON OCTOBER 12, 2015, THE CAUSE FOR BEATIFICATION FOR SERVANTS OF GOD ANTONIO CUIPA AND COMPANIONS OPENED WITH A CELEBRATION OF THE MASS. THOSE GATHERED PRAYED IN THANKSGIVING FOR THE MARTYRS WHO MADE *LA FLORIDA* HOLY, AS THEY ASKED THESE SAME MARTYRS TO CONTINUE TO GUARD THE HOLY FAITH TODAY.
YOU, OH HOLY MARTYRS, IN MEMORY OF THOSE WHO WENT BEFORE, AND IN REMEMBRANCE OF THOSE OF TODAY, PRAY FOR US, MOVE OUR HEARTS THAT SOMETIMES ARE LIKE ARID ROCKS, SO OUR LIVES MAY BE ABOUT DEDICATION AND PENANCE, AND DETACHMENT FROM THE WORLD. AND AS THE HOLY MARTYRS DIED, BURNT FOR THE HOLY FAITH, MAY WE LIVE WITH ARDENT ZEAL LIKEWISE BURNING OUR LIVES TO PREACH THE GOSPEL TO THE UNBELIEVERS.
– SERMON, FR. TOMÁS BARRIO 1731

16TH – 18TH CENTURY TIMELINE OF DISCOVERY AND EVANGELIZATION

1492 — Christopher Columbus discovers the New World

1503 — Leonardo Da Vinci begins painting the Mona Lisa

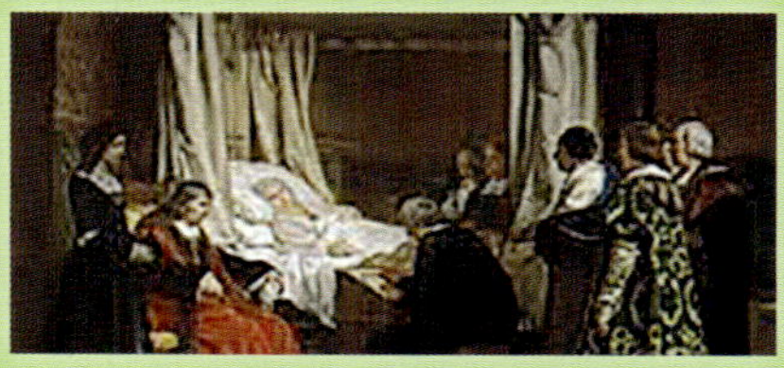

1504 — Death of Queen Isabella of Castile

1509 — Henry VIII is crowned King of England

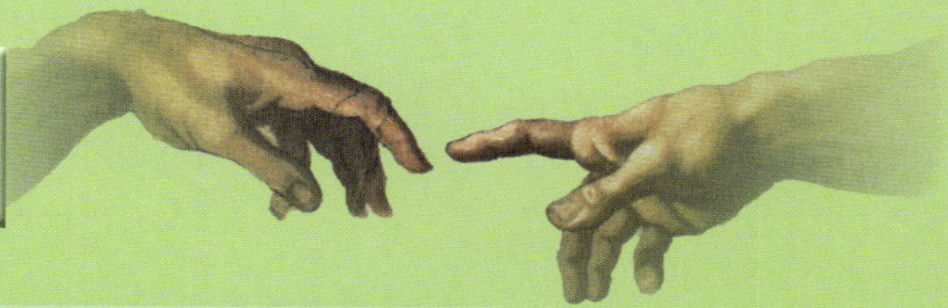

1512 — Michelangelo finishes painting the ceiling of the Sistine Chapel

1513 — Juan Ponce de León discovers Florida

1515 — St. Teresa of Avila is born

1516 — Fr. Bartolomé de las Casas, O.P. is appointed "Protector of the Indians"

1517 — Protestant Reformation begins

1519 — Hernán Cortés begins the conquest of Mexico

1521 — Ponce de León returns to Florida and is mortally wounded

The Magellan Expedition completes the first circumnavigation of the world — 1522

1526 — Lucas Vázquez de Ayllón establishes a short-lived colony in coastal Georgia

The Pánfilo de Narváez expedition lands in Tampa Bay — 1528

1531 — Our Lady of Guadalupe appears to St. Juan Diego on Tepeyac Hill (Mexico City)

English Parliament declares the king, not the pope, to be the head of the Church in England — 1534

John Calvin publishes the first edition of *Institutes of the Christian Religion* — 1536

Pope Paul III issues the encyclical, *Sublimis Deus*, forbidding the enslavement of the Indians — 1537

1539 — Hernando de Soto arrives in Tampa Bay, beginning his exploration of the Southeast

The Society of Jesus (Jesuits) is approved by Pope Paul III — 1540

1542 — Emperor Charles V issues the "New Laws" in an attempt to prevent the exploitation of natives in Spanish-held territories

1543 Copernicus proposes that the Earth revolves around the Sun

Council of Trent convenes 1545

1549 Martyrdom of Fr. Luis Cáncer and 2 other Dominicans (Tampa Bay)

1550 Debate in Valladolid (Spain) about the justice of Spanish activities in the Americas and specifically the treatment of native peoples

1552 St. Francis Xavier dies off the coast of China

1558 Queen Elizabeth I of England begins her forty-four-year reign

1559 Tristán De Luna establishes a colony in Pensacola only to be abandoned 2 years later

Council of Trent concludes 1563

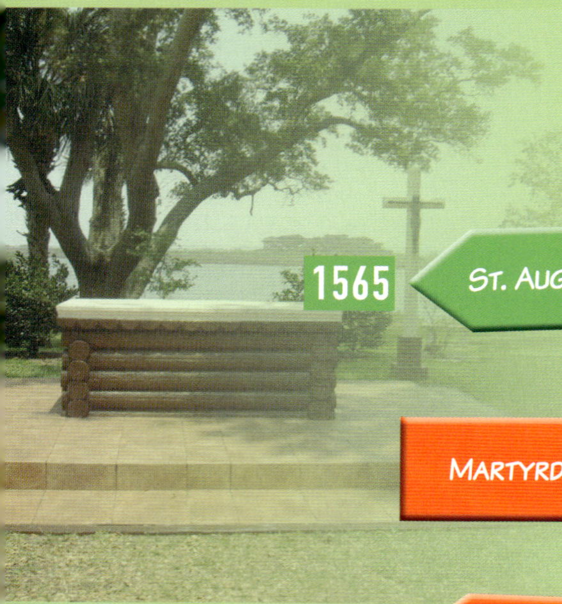

1565 St. Augustine, Florida is founded by Pedro Menéndez de Avilés

Martyrdom of Fr. Pedro Martínez, S.J. (Jacksonville)

1571 Martyrdom of Fr. Segura and 7 other Jesuits (Virginia)

1582 The Gregorian Calendar is introduced by Pope Gregory XIII

1584 St. Charles Borromeo dies in Milan

1588 Destruction of the Spanish Armada

1597 Martyrdom of Fr. Pedro de Corpa and 4 other Franciscans in Guale missions (Georgia)

1600 *Hamlet* is composed by William Shakespeare

1603 Devotion to Our Lady of La Leche is brought to Nombre de Dios (St. Augustine) from Spain

1604 Martyrdom of Fr. Marcos Garces, O.F.M. (Tallahassee)

1606 Bishop Altamirano of Cuba visits Florida where he administers the sacrament of Confirmation and also ordains priests

1607 The colony of Jamestown is founded

1611 Martyrdom of Fr. Vincente Andrade, O.F.M. (Suwannee River)

1612 Fr. Francisco Pareja, O.F.M., publishes a catechism in the Timucuan language

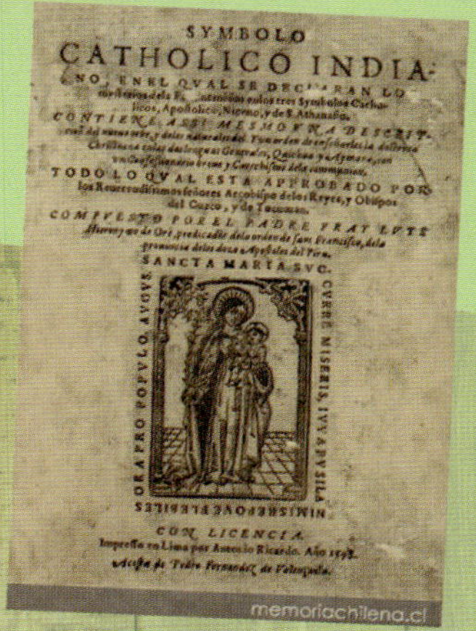

1619 Fr. Pedro Zambrano, O.F.M. establishes a mission near modern Pecos, New Mexico

1620 The Pilgrims arrive at Plymouth on the *Mayflower*

1626 St. Peter's Basilica is completed

1633 The Apalachee invite the Franciscans to establish missions among their people

1634 The *Ark* and the *Dove* arrive in Maryland bringing English Catholic settlers

1636 Harvard is founded

1646 Martyrdom of St. John de Brébeuf in Canada 3 years after the martyrdom of St. Isaac Jogues (New York)

1647 Martyrdom of 3 Franciscans, 9 Apalachee converts and the Florencia family (Tallahassee)

1661 Martyrdom of a dozen Timucua Indians (Coastal Georgia)

1670 English found settlement in Charleston

1674 Bishop Calderón of Cuba visits Florida

1676 St. Kateri Tekakwitha is baptized in a Mohawk village (New York)

1683 King Jan Sobieski of Poland defeats the Ottoman Turks at the Battle of Vienna

1689 The first Spanish mission in Texas is established

1692 The Jesuit Fr. Eusebio Kino establishes the Mission of San Xavier de Bac in Arizona

1696 Martyrdom of Fr. Luis Sánchez, O.F.M. and 2 Aypaja altar servers (Central Florida)

1697 Martyrdom of 3 Apalachee converts (Tallahassee)

1698 Martyrdom of Cipriano and Alberto (Gainesville)

1702 Col. Moore of South Carolina fails to capture St. Augustine, but several natives are martyred, including Mariana, her 9-year-old son Jacinto, and a middle-aged man named Luis

1703 Martyrdom of 3 Apalachee Indians (Tallahassee)

1704 Col. Moore's attacks resume, resulting in the destruction of the Apalchee missions, the martyrdom of Antonio Cuipa and numerous other Apalachee, 4 Franciscan friars and 1 Canarian soldier, Baltasar Francisco, and at least 3 Apalachee who were taken as slaves to Charleston

1705 Martyrdom of Fr. Agustín Ponce de León, O.F.M. and Companions (St. Augustine)

1706 Martyrdom of the Franciscans Fr. Pedro and Fr. Lucio (Pensacola), 3 native missionaries (Mobile) and Don Patricio and companions (St. Augustine)

Martyrdom of 5 Franciscans and 4 native refugees near St. Augustine over the next 7 years 1712

1715 Death of Louis XIV of France

New Orleans is founded 1718

1725 Martyrdom of 9 Yamasee Indians (St. Johns River)

Martyrdom of 6 natives including Joseph the sacristan (St. Augustine) and 3 Yamassee chiefs (St. Augustine) 1728

1732 Benjamin Franklin publishes *Poor Richard's Almanac*

Martyrdom of Chiefs Bautista, Felipe, and Anselmo and 7 others over the next 8 months (St. Augustine) 1739

1740 Siege of St. Augustine by Governor Oglethorpe of Georgia

French and Indian War begins 1756

1759 Martyrdom of Fr. Lucas de León, O.F.M. (Gainesville) and 12 Apalachee (North Florida)

1760 Martyrdom of Antonio Bendito and 4 other Chickasaw (Pensacola)

Martyrdom of 3 Apalachee protecting the Eucharist (Pensacola) 1761

1763 Florida becomes a British colony as the French and Indian War ends as most Spanish and Indian Catholics leave for Cuba

St. Junipero Serra founds the first mission in California 1769

1776 Second Continental Congress adopts the Declaration of Independence

Treaty of Paris officially ends the Revolutionary War and Florida is returned to Spain 1783

1787 The Constitutional Convention produces the United States Constitution

George Washington becomes the 1st President of the United States 1789

1793 Louis XVI and Marie Antoinette are executed during the Reign of Terror

Thomas Jefferson concludes the Louisiana Purchase 1803

1822 Florida becomes a territory of the United States

FATHER LUIS CÁNCER

FATHER PEDRO MARTÍNEZ

FATHER SEGURA AND COMPANIONS

FATHER MARCOS GARCÉS

ANTONIA DE FLORENCIA

FATHER LUIS SÁNCHEZ AND ALTAR SERVERS

MARIANA AND JACINTO

ANTONIO CUIPA

CACICA MARÍA

MANUEL

BALTASAR FRANCISCO

FATHER CRIADO AND FATHER TIBURCIO

JACINTO, JULIO AND FATHER AGUSTÍN

FATHER PEDRO AND FATHER LUCIO

DON PATRICIO

PATRICIO, DOMINGO, BENITO, MANUEL, MIGUEL, CARMELA, JULIA, VENANCIA, ERNESTO

JOSEPH

BAUTISTA

ELADIO AND ROBERTO

ANTONIO BENDITO

ELPIDIO JOSÉ, ALBERTO AND MATÍAS EL CHICO